Inner Harbor, Baltimore

Robin Levin, Photographer

IMAGE PUBLISHING, LTD.

IMAGE PUBLISHING, LTD.
1411 Hollins Street/Union Square

301 • 566-1222   Baltimore, Maryland 21223   301 • 624-5253

CREDITS
Photography by Roger Miller
Design by David Miller
Text by Ron Pilling
Edited by Margaretta H. Finn
Writing Coordinated by Sarah C. Carter
Typesetting by Delta Graphics, Inc.
Printing, color separations, and binding by Evervest Printing Co., Ltd., Hong Kong

ORDERS
For direct orders please call or write for specific cost and postage and handling to the above address. Discounts available for stores and institutions, minimum orders required.

DEDICATION
EDWARD MÜLLER & HULDA LÜDIN MÜLLER
To the memory of Edward Müller (November 16, 1862-September 2, 1925) and Hulda Lüdin Müller (April 14, 1866-September 11, 1954) my great-grandfather and great-grandmother. They were known to most everyone as Daddat and Nannan. Originally from Bubendorf, Switzerland they emigrated to the United States on February 22, 1888. I never met Daddat but I will always remember Nannan teasing and joking with my brother and me. How does one thank someone for his heritage? By remembering.

Roger Miller, 8-8-83

SPECIAL THANKS

I would like to thank everyone who had a part in this project. I would especially like to thank the following:

A special thanks to all the people and businesses of Baltimore. Without their hard work and dedication to making Baltimore the great city it is, this book would not have been possible.

I would like to thank my dedicated staff for putting up with some of the pressures we have dealt with in creating our books. Without the efforts and devotion of **Sarah C. Carter** and **Margaretta H. Finn** this book would not exist.

ROGER MILLER

Inner Harbor from Federal Hill

4   Harbor walk from south side of Inner Harbor

TABLE OF CONTENTS

Close-up of Inner Harbor from Federal Hill

INTRODUCTION

"They asked me how I knew, my true love was true..." The Oscar Hammerstein lyrics floated across the Baltimore harbor. Seated just yards from the water's edge, the audience was enraptured by the Baltimore Symphony's rendition of the famous tunes. "...I of course replied, something here inside, cannot be denied."

The melody was faint on the opposite shore, providing a perfect musical backdrop for couples on the open deck of a waterfront restaurant. At the moment the sun set that warm summer evening everything seemed to come together across the Baltimore Inner Harbor. Three large sailboats approached the dock windward of Harborplace, sails set wide on a downwind course. Lights began to twinkle everywhere, creating a glistening necklace that seemed to wrap around the waterfront.

This is Baltimore, Maryland, whose harbor just thirty years before was filled with nothing but tramp steamers and rust-streaked barges. But this evening, relaxing with a glass of wine on the waterfront deck, one could easily have argued that Baltimore is a city as romantic as Paris, as exciting as Monte Carlo, as steeped in history as Rome or Athens and as culturally rich as Vienna.

If there were a perfect vantage point from which to view three centuries of Baltimore history it may well be this spot, where patrons of the modern restaurant scan the water. Today they see the results of the Baltimore renaissance of the 1970's and 1980's which has focused on the Inner Harbor and sparked development throughout the city. In the early 1700's, however, the view included but a handful of wooden buildings clustered around the harbor, with open fields just blocks from the water. Nearby Fell's Point and Jonestown were booming ports of entry by about 1720, but both would eventually be absorbed by Baltimore as the port city grew.

It was this harbor which drew people here in the first place. Baltimore is located at the confluence of several swift running creeks which provided power for early mills throughout the fertile valleys of Baltimore County. The mills turned out goods traded by the young city's merchants, chiefly wheat and iron. As settlers moved west it became evident that Baltimore was the closest port to the Shenandoah Valley and the towns along the Ohio River. This proximity to a dynamic new manufacturing region was important. Baltimore quickly became one of the leading mercantile cities on the East Coast.

By the time of the Declaration of Independence there were over six hundred houses in Baltimore, and demand for local products spawned by the Revolutionary War spelled prosperity for the city's residents. As a shipbuilding center, Baltimore sent 250 privateers into the war against Great Britain, and local boats became the backbone of the fledgling navy. The close of the war found Baltimore poised to reap the economic benefits of independence.

But this was not the end of the new nation's difficulties with England, for in 1812 war again broke out. Once again Baltimore was the home port for many of the privateers that preyed on British shipping. The famous "Baltimore Clipper," a low-slung schooner built for speed and maneuverability, played such havoc with English ships that the city was known as the "nest of pirates" among the enemy forces.

On September 12, 1814, after burning Washington, the British army ascended the Chesapeake to teach Baltimore a lesson. A large force approached the city by land, but when their commander, General Robert Ross, was killed the British withdrew. Fort McHenry, guarding the Patapsco River entrance to the city, was soon under siege; a bombardment that would last throughout September 13. Again the defenders proved too stout-hearted, and the attack failed.

While a prisoner on a British man-of-war watching the "bombs bursting in air," Francis Scott Key penned a few lines on the back of an envelope. The next day, after his release, Key showed the poem to his brother-in-law who encouraged him to have it published. Thus was born what would become our National Anthem.

With the close of the war, Baltimoreans were again able to turn their attention to business. The most significant event of the decades before the Civil War was the founding of the Baltimore and Ohio Railroad and the beginning of railroading in America. The cornerstone for the railroad was laid on July 4, 1828, and the rail link with points westward fueled the fires of Baltimore's economic development.

The city played a tragic role in the Civil War. Baltimore was the only major city north of Washington with a decided contingent of Southern sympathizers. On April 19, 1861, the Sixth Massachusetts Infantry was passing through Baltimore when a mob of locals attacked. Four soldiers and four civilians died, the first deaths of the war. Within a month, Federal Hill was occupied by a large Federal force and Baltimore remained a city under occupation for the balance of the war.

Again Baltimore found herself in an enviable mercantile position when the war closed in 1865. By this time the city was home to 350 thousand people with more than its share of talented businessmen. There was a construction boom, fueled by a growth in population and bank deposits. Merchants like Enoch Pratt, Johns Hopkins, and Henry Walters spread their wealth over many ventures. Each eventually gave part of their good fortune back, creating colleges and universities, libraries, and museums that brought culture to the port city.

Throughout the 1800's there was a huge influx of immigrants into Baltimore, new Americans who contributed to the city's economic good fortune. Tens of thousands entered the country at Locust Point, disembarking mainly from ships out of Germany and eastern Europe. Many settled in east Baltimore, and took up the brewing or tailoring trades they had known in Europe. Their cultures somehow remained intact, creating a city that is distinctly ethnic in tone, giving modern Baltimore much of its character.

Throughout the first half of the twentieth century Baltimore continued along the same path. A major fire destroyed much of the financial district in 1904, but the city quickly rebuilt. Baltimoreans served in both world wars and, as always, Baltimore factories and ships pitched in for the war effort. But by 1950 it was obvious that the old ways, while a good foundation for the city's future, were time-worn. The wharves along Pratt and Light Streets, once bustling with both passenger traffic and cargo, were rotting derelicts. Many city neighborhoods were in rapid decline. The middle class was fleeing to the suburbs and business was following.

A group of local businessmen joined to address these problems in 1955, forming the Greater Baltimore Committee. From the beginning the idea of a partnership of public and private resources was seen as the key to future inner city development. In 1958 the concept of Charles Center was presented, and in 1961, when One Charles Center was dedicated, the Baltimore renaissance was underway.

The election of 1971 swept William Donald Schaefer into the mayoralty. Schaefer became an unabashed cheerleader for his hometown. His enthusiasm filled a gap in the city's spirit that all the new buildings along Charles Street had been unable to fill. Mayor Schaefer saw a city with a long and proud tradition, a history of indomitable courage, a strong citizenry of vast ethnic backgrounds, and a social and economic base that would be a firm foundation for future growth. He dreamed of what Baltimore could become, and slowly his dreams began to come true.

In July, 1980, the green-roofed pavilions of Harborplace opened along what twenty years earlier were abandoned wharves. The dozens of shops and restaurants in the James Rouse development, coupled with the nearby National Aquarium, the Maryland Science Center, World Trade Center and the USF Constellation attracted more visitors than Disney World that year. The Baltimore Convention Center had already opened, and that plus Harborplace inspired other development in the Inner Harbor.

Marinas have sprung up along the waterfront as far east as Canton. An impressive collection of historic ships and sailboats, as well as modern reproductions of old vessels, now calls the Inner Harbor home. The centerpiece of this floating museum is the Constellation, the first ship of the United States Navy. Built in Baltimore in 1797, the proud old frigate has the place of honor in the Inner

Harbor. The Minnie V, an authentic Chesapeake Bay skipjack, gives harbor tours under sail during the spring and summer months. In oystering season she returns to the Chesapeake to dredge oysters, as she has since the turn of the century.

The "Pride of Baltimore II", a recreated Baltimore Clipper schooner, also has her home port here. The Pride, begun in 1987 after a tragic storm sank her namesake, will sail around the world as sort of a floating ambassador, extolling the city's virtues and encouraging international partnerships.

Baltimore is quickly becoming a major boating and yachting center. Sleek powerboats and graceful sailboats have taken over the Inner Harbor, where steamboats and Chesapeake Bay working craft once tied up to pick up passengers or unload watermelons. The harbor is crowded with pleasure boats throughout the warm months and more and more captains are calling a berth at one of the harbor's new marinas their permanent home.

Where fruit and vegetable warehouses stood not long ago there are now luxury hotels and condominiums. The Gallery, sharing a building with the Stouffer Harborplace Hotel, is a four story collection of fashionable boutiques in an atrium of tinted glass. Other shops, and dozens of restaurants, have filled the streets and alleys that lead from the harbor. The Charles Street corridor has become the city's gallery district, with cafes and restaurants filling the spaces between art dealers.

So the Inner Harbor is now considered the physical heart of the city, but its spiritual center is definitely in its neighborhoods. Starting in the late 1960's, much of the renewal of Baltimore has been in places with names like Union Square, Butcher's Hill, Ridgely's Delight and Federal Hill; places where newcomers and older residents alike have restored their homes with respect to their neighborhood's past.

As neighborhood pride is rekindled in historically-significant areas, the brick fronts of the street's rowhouses are cleaned and the homes are returned to their original appearance. Most neighborhoods are made up of long, unbroken rows of brick-fronted houses, some topped with decorative cornices or embellished with ornate doorways. Baltimore was in the forefront of residential restoration when the Commission for Historical and Architectural Preservation was born in 1964. Today, CHAP oversees much of the private restoration taking place, guiding homeowners and developers alike in preserving the fine old features of the city's buildings.

Whether one lives in a narrow rowhouse in Highlandtown or in a tudor home in Roland Park, residents know their neighbors, socialize as a neighborhood, and bind together in preservation or community improvement organizations to solve problems or to enhance their surroundings. Neighborhoods sponsor block parties, ethnic festivals, and house tours and strengthen the social fabric of the city.

One reward for the work that goes on at the neighborhood level is the satisfaction of living in a city that is thriving culturally as well as economically. In Baltimore, both the performing and the visual arts are well-represented. The city sponsors a world-class symphony orchestra, whose trips to Europe and the Soviet Union have given it international acclaim. The orchestra's home is the modern Joseph Meyerhoff Symphony Hall, located in a cultural triangle that includes the Lyric Opera House, where the Baltimore Opera performs, and the Maryland Institute of Art, the country's oldest art college.

The Morris A. Mechanic Theatre presents Broadway plays and musicals, and Center Stage, near Mount Vernon Place, presents modern plays and the work of first-time playwrights as well as Shakespeare and Tennessee Williams. Repertory companies like the Vagabonds or the Spotlighters play to small audiences in converted storefronts, continuing a century-old tradition of local Baltimore theatre.

Baltimore boasts two important collections of art. Adjoining the Johns Hopkins Homewood campus is the Baltimore Museum of Art, whose Cone Collection is recognized as one of the most significant collections of modern art in the world. The Walters Art Gallery, on Mount Vernon Place, displays mostly European and Asian works. The core of the collections came to Baltimore when local merchant William Walters, and his son Henry, created the museum from their private collections.

The Walters is in the shadow of the Washington Monument, on Mount Vernon Place. The monument

Inner Harbor at sunset from Marina

was completed in 1829 in an area that was then so rural the city fathers felt secure that should it topple, the monument would do little damage. It was the first important monument to the Father of the Country, and has since been joined by monuments to soldiers in every war (including both sides in the Civil War), Christopher Columbus, and virtually every personage ever to have called Baltimore home.

Baltimore is, after all, a city that refuses to forget her past. The history of living in Baltimore is displayed in the Baltimore City Life Museums, a collection that includes the venerable Peale Museum, the Carroll Mansion, and a restored working class house of about 1840 housing the Urban Archaeology Museum. The Maryland Historical Society is the major repository of important Maryland furniture, silver, and works of art. Homes of Babe Ruth, Edgar Allan Poe, and Baltimore writer H.L. Mencken are open to the public. Other museums display everything from a turn-of-the century oyster packing house to the locomotives that pulled our earliest trains.

There's a long history of professionalism in sports in Baltimore that continues unabated. As early as 1869 there was a professional baseball team here, the Baltimore Orioles. The modern Orioles opened their first season in 1954 and have since put together one of the strongest winning traditions in the game. Memorial Stadium is still the team's home, though a new ball park is on the drawing boards for the Camden Station area near the Inner Harbor.

The Baltimore Blast, the city's entrant in the Major Indoor Soccer League, plays its season in the Baltimore Arena as do the Skipjacks, Baltimore's professional ice hockey team. On local ice rinks, softball diamonds and fields across town there are amateur teams that play in Baltimore leagues for fans who prefer to participate rather than watch from the sidelines. The Maryland state sport, jousting, is popular in horse country just north and west of the city.

Throughout the year there is thoroughbred racing at the area's many race tracks. The season peaks in May, when the Preakness, Baltimore's jewel in horse racing's Triple Crown, is run at Pimlico Race Track.

Without a firm economic footing, however, none of the Baltimore renaissance would have been possible. It takes more than tourists and a baseball team to propel a city into the twenty-first century, and local business has learned to adapt to the changing mercantile environment. Baltimore's backbone, since the very earliest days, has always been the port, and the modern Port of Baltimore is still a major center of trade. Through the combined efforts of private trading companies and the Maryland Port Administration, the port's facilities have been modernized and its services are marketed internationally.

Other industries take advantage of Baltimore's educational and financial assets. Partnerships with the University of Maryland, Johns Hopkins University and the private sector have resulted in jobs in industries that didn't exist thirty years ago, notably in high technology and bio-technological research. As growth in these new fields increases the demand for financial service also grows. Baltimore is home to five major trust companies as well as firms in the insurance and bonding fields, and as a result is the focal point of regional finance.

So Baltimore, with an eye to its past and clear goals in its future, is prepared to enter its fourth century on the Patapsco River. The face of the city has changed often and will undoubtedly look much different in years to come. But adaptability has never been a problem in this town which has endured a national revolution and enemy bombardment, has been split by a civil war and nearly burned to the ground, and finally has seen its economic base change dramatically. However, much will always be the same. Baltimore is a city with an understanding of how its history has brought it this far, a city that continues to prosper with a solid foundation of three hundred years of heritage.

Aerial view of Inner Harbor

INNER HARBOR

Strolling along in front of Harborplace

Top: Crowd watching street performers in front of Harborplace
Bottom: The U.S. Frigate Constellation, overlooking Harborplace's Pratt Street Pavillion

Top: Harbor walk in front of Harborplace
Bottom: Inside Harborplace's Light Street Pavillion

World Trade Center towering over Harborplace

Boats crowding Inner Harbor

Actors performing in front of the Light Street Pavilion

The Gallery at Harborplace, a new mall across
from the Pratt Street Pavilion

Inside The National Aquarium in Baltimore

Outside The National Aquarium

The Davis Planetarium at the Maryland Science Center

The silver IMAX theater, a new addition to the Maryland Science Center

Top: Some of the entertainment at Harbor Lights
Bottom: Harbor Lights Pavilion

Boat Marina at the Inner Harbor

Preakness Balloon Festival at Druid Hill Park

ENTERTAINMENT & RECREATION

The John Eager Howard Room at the Hotel Belvedere

The Omni Inner Harbor Hotel

The Sheraton Inner Harbor Hotel

Top: The Hyatt Regency Hotel
Bottom: The Stouffer Harborplace Hotel

Top: The Baltimore Marriott — Inner Harbor Hotel
Bottom: Dining at Hampton's, at The Harbor Court Hotel

Haussner's, the unique restaurant on Eastern Avenue

Top: Dining at the Conservatory atop the Peabody Court Hotel
Bottom: The Prime Rib Restaurant

Top: The Duck Pond at the Baltimore Zoo
Bottom: A Giraffe at the Baltimore Zoo

Top: September's annual Baltimore City Fair
Bottom: The Baltimore Streetcar Museum

The Block, home of Baltimore's notorious burlesque shows

P.T. Flaggs, located in the Power Plant

Statue of the Marquis de Lafayette,
Peabody Conservatory in background, Mount Vernon

HISTORIC MONUMENTS

Washington Monument with cherry blossoms, Mount Vernon

Aerial view of Fort McHenry

Period Reenactment, Circa 1812, Fort McHenry

Top: Roundhouse Interior, B & O Railroad Museum, Mount Clare
Bottom: Roundhouse Exterior, B & O Railroad Museum, Mount Clare

Baltimore Shot Tower

Top: Mount Clare Mansion, Carroll Park
Bottom: Restored interior, Mount Clare Mansion, Carroll Park

Top: Babe Ruth Birthplace Museum and
Orioles Baseball Museum, Ridgely's Delight
Bottom: The Peale Museum, across from City Hall

The Baltimore Arts Tower, commonly known as
the Bromo Seltzer Tower, Metro Center

Edgar Allan Poe House, Amity Street

Period Recreation, Maryland Historical Society,
Mount Vernon

Flag House, just outside of Little Italy

The City from Federal Hill